MARKETING RESEARCH

Introduction to Marketing Research for Business Students

Including case study - Coca Cola: The New Coke Debacle

Mario Chinas

Chinas, Mario.
Marketing Research: Introduction to Marketing Research for Business Students - 2nd ed.
Includes bibliographical references and index.
ISBN: 978-9925-7383-0-4

Webpage: https://www.mccebooks.com

TABLE OF CONTENTS

PREFACE

Welcome to the 2nd edition of *Marketing Research: Introduction to Marketing Research for Business Students.*

This book aims to introduce Marketing Research by providing the fundamental theory of the topic in question in a clear and concise manner.

It covers the basic fundamentals of *Marketing Research*, and moves on to discuss the Research Process, via the example of case study - The case of New Coke. We then conclude on the case study and the importance of *Marketing Research* & the Research process.

Our series of Books for Business Students are concise and targeted to maximizing your 'value for time', i e to give you the maximum essential learning on the subject matter in the shortest time.

As you will notice, our Books are written in a style and format that emulates essay writing. The aim is to familiarise you, the reader, with the format and style expected in essay writing, providing a bridge between the study material and the output you will be expected to deliver in your essay projects and essay based exams. Moreover they provide a wealth of references / bibliography, saving you valuable time that you can utilise to further enhance your work.

Follow us on Pinterest (Pinner- Mccebooks) and Twitter (@MCCebooks) for continuous new material (articles, study material, etc) for your studies.

Visit our Facebook page (MCCebooks), Like and Follow for updates and to receive special offers and FREE material!

Visit my Amazon Author page for further details on all my Books & eBooks
http://www.amazon.com/Mario-Chinas/e/B00PCN1WFC/

NOTE - *BLAST FROM THE PAST* - THE COCA COLA DEBACLE

This is, or should be, a legendary marketing failure of epic scale. New Coke was the reformulation of Coca-Cola introduced on April 23, 1985 to replace the original formula of Coca-Cola (also called Coke).

The American public's reaction to the change was so negative that the original formula was reintroduced as "Coca-Cola Classic", while the new formula was eventually re-branded as "Coke II".

Bottles and cans continued to bear the "Coca-Cola Classic" title until 2009 when the company announced that it would discontinue the use of "Classic" to avoid confusion with the younger generation.

Note that Coca-Cola Classic differed from the original formula in that it uses high fructose corn syrup instead of cane sugar to sweeten the drink. So in fact the original coke formula is no more!

INTRODUCTION

Even though Research is a fundamental concept, there is no consensus on its definition. The Longman Dictionary of Contemporary English (1981, p. 940) defines research as the 'advanced study of a subject, so as to learn new facts or scientific laws'. Hussey & Hussey (1997) and Saunders et al (2009) describe research as a systematic and methodical process of inquiry and investigation through which an increase in knowledge occurs.

The purpose of marketing research is to gather information which will allow an organisation to make better and more informed decisions. 'Marketing research is the function that links consumer, customer and public to the market through information – information used to identify and define marketing opportunities and problems; generate refine and evaluate marketing actions; monitor marketing performance; and improve understanding of marketing as a process' (American Marketing Association).

Put differently, marketing research is the planning, collection, and analysis of data relevant to marketing decision making, and the transition of the results of this analysis in an appropriate format to the management.

Here it is useful to point out that marketing research is different to market research. Market research is the collection and analysis of data from a sample of individuals, relating to their characteristics, behaviour, opinions etc. As we have seen, marketing research looks into marketing strategy problems with an aim to help an organisation to make better and more informed decisions.

Marketing research can be classified into various categories, and different authors make different classifications. One useful approach is to separate marketing research into Problem Identification Research that will provide information about the marketing environment and helps diagnose a problem, and Problem Solving Research that will solve specific marketing problems.

Whatever the type of research, there is a fundamental framework for the research process to be followed. The precise number of stages varies from textbook to textbook, but they include 'formulating and clarifying a topic, reviewing the literature, designing the research, collecting data, analyzing data and writing up' (Saunders et al, 2009, p. 10). As any type of research, Marketing Research follows the above research framework.

A simple and commonly used structure in Business Research is the framework described by Hussey & Hussey (1997). The framework comprises of six steps to be followed in sequence, although it should be kept in mind that at any stage you may need to reconsider your decisions and return to an earlier stage. The six steps of the research process are:
1. Identify the research topic – the general subject that you wish to investigate.

2. Defining the research problem – This may sound at first as identical to the above but it is not. At this stage you narrow down the topic to a particular problem / question to be investigated.
3. Determining how to conduct the study – The approach to be used in conducting the research; the research paradigm and design. At the most basic level, you need to decide if your research will be quantitative or qualitative.
4. Collecting the research data – choosing the appropriate data collection methods.
5. Analyzing and interpreting the research data – transforming data into information through which conclusions can be reached.
6. Writing the report – Presenting your work in an appropriate format.

In Hussey & Hussey (2009) the steps have been revised; although the number of steps has remained unchanged, the following amendments have been made to steps (1) and (2):
1. Choose a topic and search the literature – A scan of the literature for previous studies on the same topic has been added, to help focus your ideas on a particular research problem.
2. Review the literature and define the research problem / question – Following from the previous step, a review of the literature has been added in order to identify any gaps which will indicate original areas of research that you may pursue.

The remaining steps have slight alterations but in essence remain unchanged. An almost identical framework for the marketing research process comprising of six steps is provided by Malhotra (2010), while Wilson (2006) provides a very similar seven step framework (separating the collection of secondary and primary data).

Saunders et al (2009) proposes an eight step framework for conducting research. The main differences in comparison to the Six Step framework by Hussey & Hussey are that the literature is considered in a separate step and the issues of negotiating access and addressing ethical issues, which Hussey & Hussey deal with separately under practical issues in conducting research, are a step in their own right. We can therefore conclude that the steps are more or less agreed upon in the literature and it is their presentation that differs from author to author.

THE RESEARCH PROCESS - THE CASE OF NEW COKE

We will examine the stages of the Research Process through the example of a famous marketing blunder; the introduction in 1985 of NEW COKE by COCA COLA. In examining the stages of the Research Process we will make use of the original Six Step Framework by Hussey & Hussey (1997).

IDENTIFY THE RESEARCH TOPIC

In identifying a research topic the researcher generates and refines research ideas. Once the general topic has been chosen the researcher must sort through the broad research topic to clarify a precise set of ideas or concepts. The research topic may be suggested by a problem or issue that has arisen.

However, in choosing a research topic certain common sense issues need to be kept in mind. The capability of the researcher to investigate the matter may sound obvious, but must be considered before proceeding. The researcher has a set of skills & knowledge; more skills & knowledge can be acquired but this will require time and commitment. The researcher must ensure that either he/she already has the necessary skills & knowledge or that acquiring them is achievable. For example learning a statistical package (eg. SPSS) for the purposes of a research project is more realistic than having to learn a foreign language! Another issue is that of access to the necessary data. The research topic may be fascinating but if you cannot access the necessary data then it is an unviable proposition. Moreover the access to the data must be legitimate and obtained in an ethical manner.

In the case of Coca Cola the research topic arose from the erosion of its market position. Thus the broad research topic was its market position. More specifically -

- The previous 15 years saw Coca-Cola's market share remain flat while Pepsi's continued to climb.
- Coke's market share fell from 24.3 in 1980 to 21.8 in 1984.
- Coke was trailing in supermarkets by 1.7 percent, which represented a third of coke's total sales
- Coke felt that it was in danger of becoming the #2 soft drink

Coca Cola had both the capability and the access to information (eg. publicly available secondary information and access to consumers and other stakeholders for conducting primary research).

DEFINING THE RESEARCH PROBLEM

In defining the problem, the researcher should take into account the aim of the research, any relevant background information, what outcome information is needed and how it will be used in decision making (Malhotra, 2010). In order to define the problem, interviews with management or other relevant staff may be required, as well as input from experts in the particular field. Additionally there may be a need for some qualitative research such as focus groups in order to gain a better understanding of the problem under investigation. Saunders et al (2009) suggest that at this stage a preliminary study may be in order (defined as a review of some literature and the use of techniques such as those mentioned above, i.e. interviews, focus groups, etc). The precise definition of the problem 'aids in understanding the information that will be needed and therefore helps in identifying the research objectives' (Wilson, 2006, p. 21).

In the early 1980s, regular Coke (the drink) was steadily losing market share to Pepsi-Cola. From the information readily available to the management of Coca Cola they were aware that Diet Coke had cannibalized Coke sales but another reason for the fall was that Pepsi had successfully positioned Pepsi-Cola for the youth market and was winning a greater share of new cola drinkers than Coke was (Henning, 2009).

Furthermore, Pepsi-Cola was reported to taste better. Since the 1970s, Pepsi had introduced the Pepsi Challenge – testing consumers blind on the difference between its own brand and Coca Cola. To the horror of Coca-Cola most of those who participated preferred Pepsi's sweeter formula (Bastedo & Davis, 1993). As the success of Diet Coke indicated, the market was leaning toward sweeter drinks.

Since Coca Cola outstripped Pepsi in advertising and distribution, the problem, as Coca-Cola perceived it, came down to the product itself. As the Pepsi Challenge had highlighted millions of times over, Coke could always be defeated when it came down to taste (Kennedy, 2011). As the head of market research for Coca-Cola USA, Roy Stout, had famously said "why are we losing share? You look at the Pepsi Challenge, and you have to begin asking about taste." (Bastedo & Davis, 1993). They focused on measuring taste preference rather than buying intentions based on the consumers perception of the product.

Thus the research problem was defined as the improvement of the current Coke formula. Through this move the Coca-Cola Company intended to re-energize its Coca-Cola brand and the cola category in its largest market, the United States (The Coca-Cola Company, [online]). It seems that the management did not understand how people perceived Coca Cola (much more than just taste), and based their definition of the problem on their myopic view without sufficient information and understanding. Someone could surmise that they had no understanding of their customer base, and did not follow basic principles to define the problem, due to their overconfidence.

DETERMINING HOW TO CONDUCT THE STUDY

Once the researcher has defined what needs to be studied, a blueprint for how to conduct the research must be set. This blueprint, usually referred to as the Research design, details the procedures necessary for obtaining the required information (Malhotra, 2010). Decisions need to be made on what data will be collected and why, where and how it will be collected, and how the data will be analyzed in order to answer the research question.

However, before constructing the Research Design, the research philosophy / paradigm, must be chosen. The choice of research philosophy will reflect the researchers basic beliefs; the way in which he/she views the world (Hussey & Hussey, 1997, and Saunders et al, 2009). Of course the research question, and thus the aim of the research, may also affect the choice of research philosophy.

The literature on research philosophy and design is vast and out of the scope of this paper. However the important thing to note is that choices have to be made on the theoretical foundations on which the research will be built.

In the case of Coca Cola a new, improved (better liked) recipe for coca cola needed to be identified. First it was up to the technical division to formulate new recipes for coca cola and then Marketing research needed to test them.

The technical division brewed a formula of Coke that beat Pepsi in blind taste - tests, by as much as 6 to 8 points. Before, Pepsi had beaten Coke by 10 to 15 points. This was an 18 - point swing.

Coca Cola used a survey / taste tests of nearly 200,000 consumers to test the new Coke. Focus groups were also used to test consumer reactions to the new Coke, but these were done after and not before the survey (Kennedy, 2011; and *Bastedo* & Davis, 1993).

RESEARCH DESIGN - REPORT STRUCTURE

Below we present a template structure for a Research design report. This is just a guideline, the actual design report structure may differ depending on the needs of the actual case.

Executive summary – Overview of the objectives of this research, who will perform the work, when, and by what means / resources and limitations.

Preface/background – Detail any relevant information or previous research that has been completed in relation to this work.

Objectives – Define the goals of this work.

Research methods & Data analysis – Define what sort of research methods will be utilised, the reasoning for using these approaches and the data analysis to be performed. More than one option may be described here, leaving the final decision to the management.

Reporting – Provide an outline of the expected information to be presented in the outcome, and a schedule for the report.

Resources – Estimated costings, man hours, time considerations.

Summary / Recommendations – Propose specific research methods or summarise the options that need to be considered, the timing and the resources to be used (under each option if several options are presented), justifying your recommendations.

COLLECTING THE RESEARCH DATA

Data collection is the process of putting into practice the research design. Depending on the type of research it involves measuring variables, counting occurrences, recording behavior, etc. In marketing research it involves the fieldwork required to perform the data collection method(s), for example by performing interviews. This may sound simple but it requires a lot of planning as the people that will collect the data need to be trained, the material needs to be prepared (eg. questionnaires), a sample must be selected using the set sampling method, etc. Furthermore, the data collection methods will need to be checked and tested to ensure that the data collection is successful.

In the case of Coca Cola the company already had a trained workforce at its disposal and a well structure Marketing Division to plan and execute the data collection. In taste testing a new Coke formula, Coca Cola Company used three different formulations, which it tested against traditional Coke and Pepsi, using a random sample of 200,000 consumers who took the test. No further reliable information regarding the focus groups is available.

ANALYZING AND INTERPRETING THE RESEARCH DATA

After data has been collected from a representative sample the next step is to analyze and interpret the data. The objective at this stage in the research process is dependent on the type of research. For example a researcher with a predictive research purpose using a survey approach will be trying to prove or disprove the research question. Variations throughout the research process including research purpose have a major effect on how data is analyzed.

Coca-Cola found that people preferred the new Coke formula over both the original Coke and Pepsi (Clifford S., 2009). Based on this finding the switch to the new Coke proceeded. After 99 years with essentially the same taste, Coca-Cola decided to switch to a new taste, based purely on the results of blind taste tests.

However, the research had focused on taste alone rather than brand preference. And when taste testers blindly chose New Coke over original Coke, they were never told that New Coke would ultimately replace the original (Fisher, 1985, and Mathews, 2005).

WRITING THE REPORT

Finally the information produced through the analysis of the data needs to be presented in a meaningful way. In presenting the results of a quantitative approach, the aim would be to discuss the extent to which the results either prove or disprove the research question. In qualitative research the discussion would present the meanings that emerge from the data.

In the case of Coca Cola we are not told exactly how the results were presented, but it is reasonable to assume that the results of the taste testing were presented to management in some summary format (e.g. charts) showing that the new taste was preferred over the original taste and Pepsi.

NEW COKE - THE RESULT

On April 23, New Coke was launched in the US with fanfare, including prime-time TV ads. Company Chairman Roberto C. Goizueta proclaimed New Coke "smoother, rounder yet bolder," (Ross, 2005).

Public reaction in the US was overwhelmingly negative; some people likened the change in Coke to trampling the American flag. Soon people were stockpilling cases of the old coke. A Hollywood producer, reportedly rented a wine cellar to hold 100 cases of the old Coke. On July 11nth 1985, Coca-Cola recalled New Coke from store shelves. "We did not understand the deep emotions of so many of our customers for Coca-Cola," said company President Donald R. Keough (Ross, 2005).

The return of original formula Coca-Cola, put the cap on 79 days that revolutionized the soft-drink industry. "We set out to change the dynamics of sugar colas in the United States, and we did exactly that -- albeit not in the way we had planned," then chairman and chief executive officer Roberto Goizueta said in 1995 at a special employee event honoring the 10-year anniversary of "new Coke." The events of 1985 changed forever the dynamics of the soft-drink industry and the success of The Coca-Cola Company, as the Coca-Cola brand soared to new heights and consumers continued to remember the love they have for Coca-Cola (The Coca Cola Company, 2012).

CONCLUSION

Market research provides the means via which data is collected and analyzed to provide management with in-depth information for making marketing decisions. With effective market research, an organisation can gain invaluable information about its environment, such as demographics, competition, market trends, economic conditions and the spending habits of customers. You may want to think of the PESTEL Framework and Porter's Five Forces Model.

The research process is a framework aimed at guiding the researcher through the process of conducting a successful research. It begins with clearly defining the problem to be investigated, developing an approach and formulating the research design, collecting the data, analyzing and presenting the results.

The lesson to be learned from the Coca Cola example is that each stage needs to be performed methodically and meticulously. No matter how many resources you have at your disposal, if proper attention is not paid at each step the results may lead to a wrong decision.

In the case of Coca Cola two possible mistakes were made. Firstly, at the stage of defining the research problem the secondary information was not interpreted correctly. Coca Cola took for granted the results of the Pepsi Challenge. However, they failed to take into account that the test was carried out on random samples of consumers in malls, some of whom were not cola drinkers. Moreover, the test was limited to taste, which is just one element of the overall consumer perception of the product (Imran, 1999). Secondly, Coca Cola assumed that people would want a better tasting Coke; they did not research if this was the case. A qualitative study, possibly using focus groups should have been done first. Instead focus groups were used following the survey, more like an afterthought, to test reactions to the new taste and confirm the survey results. The remainder of the research answered the research question; but the question was the wrong question.

If anything, the above tells us that nothing should be taken for granted. A researcher should start with a blank page and build the research methodically without making assumptions. Otherwise, even the best can get it wrong!

REFERENCES

1. Bastedo M. & Davis A, 1993. God, What a Blunder: The New Coke Story. Available from: http://www.colafountain.co.uk/newcoke.htm (30/11/11)

2. Clifford S., 2009. Coca-Cola Deleting 'Classic' From Coke Label. The New York Times, 31 Jan 2009 p. B2. Available from: http://www.nytimes.com/2009/01/31/business/media/31coke.html (05/12/11)

3. Fisher A. (1985). Coke's Brand Loyalty Lesson, Fortune, 05 Aug 1985, p.44-46

4. Henning J., 2009. Coke, New Coke & the Angry Focus Group. Vovici Corporation. Available from: http://blog.vovici.com/blog/bid/18094/Coke-New-Coke-the-Angry-Focus-Group (03/12/11)

5. Hussey J. & Hussey R., 1997. Business Research: A practical Guide for Undergraduate & Postgraduate Students. London: Macmillan

6. Hussey J. & Hussey R., 2009. Business Research: A practical Guide for Undergraduate & Postgraduate Students. New York : Palgrave Macmillan

7. Imram N. (1999). The role of visual cues in consumer perception and acceptance of a food product. Nutrition & Food Science. 99:5, p.224 – 230

8. Longman Group, 1981. The Longman Dictionary of Contemporary English. Harlow: Longman

9. Kennedy E., 2011. Coke Case Study. Available from:
    http://www.reading.ac.uk/web/FILES/inform/Coke_Case_Study
    _Workshop_Task_EK.pdf (03/12/11).

10. Matthews B., 2005. Coca-cola's Big Mistake: New Coke 20
    Years Later. New York 10. Available online:
    http://newyork10.cityspur.com/2009/12/coca-colas-big-
    mistake-new-coke-20-years-later/ (06/12/2011)

11. Malhotra N, 2010. Marketing Research: An applied
    orientation, 6th edition. Upper Sadler River, New Jersey:
    Prentice Hall.

12. Ross M. (2005). It seemed like a good idea at the time.
    msnbc.com. Available from:
    http://www.msnbc.msn.com/id/7209828/ns/us_news/t/it-
    seemed-good-idea-time/#.TtKolFaKkbc (03/12/11).
    also, http://www.nbcnews.com/id/7209828/ns/us_news/t/it-
    seemed-good-idea-time/#.WhH6sEqWblU

13. Saunders M., Lewis P. & Thornhill A., 2009. Research
    Methods for Business Students, 5th edition. Harlow: Pearson

14. The Coca Cola Company. Coke Lore: The Real Story of New
    Coke. The Coca Cola Company. Available from:
    http://www.thecoca-
    colacompany.com/heritage/cokelore_newcoke.html (01/12/11)
    also at
    http://www.coca-colacompany.com/stories/coke-lore-new-coke

15. Wilson A. (2006). Marketing Research: An Integrated
    Approach, 2nd edition. Harlow: Pearson

I hope you have enjoyed Marketing Research: Introduction to Marketing Research for Business Students.

For any suggestions or comments please email us at info@mccebooks.com

INDEX

Index pages are accurate for 6" by 8" inch page and Arial font size 11

OTHER BOOKS BY THE AUTHOR

EFFICIENT MARKET HYPOTHESIS: Introduction to the Efficient Market Hypothesis for Business Students

VISION AND MISSION: Introduction to Vision and Mission for Business Students

PERCEPTION: Introduction to Perception for Business Students

BUSINESS ESSAY WRITING: A student's guide to coursework via theory and practical examples

QUESTIONNAIRES: Short Guide to Questionnaire Design for Business Students

PROJECT MANAGEMENT: Introduction to Project Management for Business Students

GROUPS IN ORGANISATIONS: Introduction to Work Groups for Business Students

Visit our webpage for the full range of Books and purchase options.

Webpage: https://www.mccebooks.com

MARKETING RESEARCH

Introduction to Marketing Research for Business Students

Including case study - Coca Cola: The New Coke Debacle

ISBN 978-9925-7383-0-4

SECOND EDITION

www.ingramcontent.com/pod-product-compliance
Lightning Source LLC
Chambersburg PA
CBHW022058190326
41520CB00008B/807